THE LONGING LUTE

PROF. M.U. MALKANI
T.H. ADVANI

THE LONGING LUTE

PROF. M.U. MALKANI AND T.H. ADVANI

SECOND EDITION: DECEMBER 2024

ISBN No. 978-93-341-4783-4

WRITER, DESIGNER, AND PUBLISHER: KABIR MALKANI

EDITOR: GINA MALKANI

COPYWRITING CONSULTANT: SAI VAIDYA

ACKNOWLEDGEMENTS: *Dr. Qasim Rajpar* for consenting to the reuse of his content, *Mohan Madhosh* for his support and encouragement, and *Manju Gulrajani* for her help with translating the *Sindhi* quote on the last page.

DISCLAIMER: *The Longing Lute* is a collection of poems written by *Prof. M.U. Malkani* and his friend *T.H. Advani*. It was first published for limited circulation at *Kohinoor Printing Works, Karachi,* in the early 1920s. The original edition, and quite possibly the only surviving copy of this book, was in the possession of *Prof. M.U. Malkani's* nephew, *Hiroo Alimchand Malkani,* and eventually handed down by inheritance, to his children, *Gina* and *Kabir,* who have taken the initiative to publish this second edition. Publication details of the aforementioned edition, such as the publication date, print run, distributorship, and circulation figures, are unknown. There is also no information on the existence of this book, or its contents having been previously published and available in general circulation in any form—print, audio, video, or digital, whatsoever. Everyone that has contributed towards this endeavour is either a direct or indirect descendant of *Prof. M.U. Malkani*. All efforts to trace the lineage of the co-poet, *T.H. Advani,* or the proprietors of *Kohinoor Printing Works, Karachi,* were unsuccessful up to and at the time of publishing. Every effort has been taken to preserve the poetry and the language in its original intended form, and great care has been taken to avoid errors or omissions. Context to native terms has been included using subtext where necessary. The publisher holds neither liability nor accountability towards any person or entity claiming ownership of the title or the contents herein.

WARNING: No part of this publication may be reproduced, distributed, or transmitted in any form or by any means, including photocopying, recording, or other electronic or mechanical methods, or by any information storage and retrieval system without the prior written permission of the publisher, except in the case of very brief quotations embodied in critical reviews and certain other non-commercial uses permitted by international copyright law.

Copyright © Kabir Malkani 2024

WITH SPECIAL THANKS TO

ANJALI MALKANI
DIANA SEN
POONAM WHITE
SHALINI MIRCHANDANI
SUMANGALA HINDMARSH

In Loving Memory Of
Prof. Mangharam Udharam Malkani
1896—1980

Foreword

The first edition of *The Longing Lute* was written over a century ago in *Sindh*, in pre-partition India, during the *British Raj*. Generally recognized for his penmanship in *Sindhi*, this unique initiative by *Prof. M.U. Malkani*, is written in English, and not set in prose. The *Preface* establishes this joint venture with his dear friend *T.H. Advani* to have been a minor experiment to seek critique, appreciation, and intellectual indulgence, from their peer group, and sets the precedence for the manifestation of this masterpiece.

Through their captivating words, the poets explore the intricate tapestry of love and its power to evoke opposing yet inseparable ideas of happiness and heartache. Various metaphors of nature, seasons, music, and spirituality have been juxtaposed against the range of emotions one experiences in the pursuit of a soulmate. This universal theme of love and longing resonates deeply with one and all and has been articulated with great simplicity and eloquence.

This second edition has been published to preserve and extend the legacy of these writers and share their poetic genius with a wider readership, which it so richly deserves. In preserving these timeless verses, we invite readers to experience the enduring power of language that transcends time and echoes emotions—both personal and profound.

To

One who knows,

&

The other who knows not.

Opinions

JUL 1923 – "The best thing you have written is undoubtedly *'The Rose and its Thorns'*. Here you have quite a good idea well expressed."

JAN 1924 – "You are making progress in English verse so demanding and receiving criticism of a higher standard."

JAN 1925 – "You have written a sonnet quite remarkable *'At the Double-Door'*. It is vivid, beautifully couched in tender language and clear. Its lines are picturesque. Then again in the lyric *'For Ever, and for Ever'* is stuff of the same sort, and the workmanship of it is good."

*Opinions are anonymous, as in the original edition.

Preface

In presenting this little volume to a small circle of our literary friends, we must confess we have been principally influenced by the vanity of seeing ourselves in print, although not a little encouraged by the appreciation and guidance of the Editor of *Great Thoughts.

We crave the indulgence of the readers to judge these verses sympathetically: bearing in mind the fact that the expression of native ideas in a foreign tongue—with its idiosyncrasies of idiom, and its subtleties of poetic rhythm—is, to say the least, rather a presumptuous performance.

It might be mentioned that the writers of these verses have been intellectual companions all their youth, and have read, thought, and written at the same time—almost together. Hence the desirability of a joint venture, in which the poems of the two have been promiscuously interspersed; – intending to present a little literary curiosity to the reader: that of distinguishing the individual genius of the two writers. By the way of a clue to this end, it might be suggested that the two companion poems *"'Twas only a Rose"* and *"The Beauty of the Rose"* written coincidentally on the same theme, are respectively by T.H. Advani and M.U. Malkani.

*No context provided by the poets while referencing 'Great Thoughts'.

"One speck of pollen ere my petals close, – Bring me one touch of love before I die."

Laurence Hope

"My time for flower-gathering is over; and through the dark night, I have not the rose, only the pain remains."

Rabindranath Tagore

Table of Contents

THE UNRESPONDED CALL.. 19
THE PILGRIMAGE OF LOVE.. 20
THE LASS I LOVE.. 21
"I'LL MELT AND MINGLE IN MY LOVE"................................... 23
SPRING BLOSSOMS.. 24
BUT TO LOOK UPON... 25
BEFORE THE GRANTH SAHIB.. 26
IN THE SKIES... 27
FRAGMENTS... 29
THE CRESCENT AND THE STAR... 30
DAILY GIFTS.. 31
ON SEEING A CLAY-RELIEF OF RADHA AND KRISHNA............ 32
WITHDRAWN... 33
THE PARROTS ON THE PEEPUL TREE... 34
THE RURAL NYMPH.. 35
THE END.. 37
THE SEARCH.. 38
TO THE TWINKLING STAR... 39
THE FORLORN FLUTE... 40
"'TWAS ONLY A ROSE"... 41
THE BEAUTY OF THE ROSE... 42
ON THE COMING OF THE RAIN... 43
AFTER THE RAIN... 44
EYES NEED EYES.. 45
YOUTH AND BEAUTY... 46
LONELINESS.. 47

IF I WERE THE SEA	48
THE BREEZE AND THE CLOUD	50
LOTUS BLOOMS	51
ASPIRATION	53
A LULLABY	54
THE HULLER'S SONG	55
RIFT IN THE LUTE	56
THE SWALLOW ON THE LAKE	57
THE POET'S SOUL	59
THE MOON-LIT STREAM	61
ACROSS THE SEA	62
TILL YOU ARRIVE	63
MUSIC WAILS	64
THE BIRD AND THE BEAST	65
THE ROSE AND ITS THORNS	66
THE SIMPLEST THINGS	67
THE INITIATED DEVOTEE	68
A CUP OF COCOA	69
A HARLOT'S HEART	70
LOVE'S PHILOSOPHY	71
AT THE DOUBLE-DOOR	72
"FOR EVER, AND FOR EVER"	73
"HOW BEAUTEOUS IS THE WORLD, YET OH HOW LONELY"	74

The Unresponded Call

I've called to Love times out of number,
    But save the wild howl of the wind,
When all the world lies deep in slumber,
    No answer comes back that is kind.

I've wheedled and coaxed and entreated,
    And waited through long years, confined;
But all hopes have till now been cheated,
    For no answer e'er comes that is kind.

The stars too to-night are all waiting,
    For their mistress, the moon, yet behind;
And she'll rise though a bit she be late in,
    But her answer will ne'er be unkind.

Will I, Love, be waiting for ever,
    No rapture in thee ever find?......
But save the wind's howl ceasing never,
    No answer I hear that is kind.

The Pilgrimage of Love

O, would I went far, far away,
    Away in the west, as the sun goes down,
Where lives my Love across the sea,
    And where the sun sinks red and brown.

Across the moor, across the plain,
    Across the stretching fields of corn,
I walk and walk on far away,
    With dreaminess from morn to morn;

Along the river-bank, and then
    I follow its course to the sea;
And then along the sea-beach sands,
    To my Love, with my heart and me.

In noon-day sun, 'mid scorching sands,
    Slaked throat athirst, and tongue parched dry,
My weary steps plod on and on,
    Without a groan, without a sigh.

With drooping limbs, till I arrive,
    Where lives my Love across the sea;
And there I fall and faint away,
    At my Love's feet in painful glee.

I open my dim eyes, and I see,
My Love by my side, nursing me;
    I clasp her to my drooping heart:
"Sweet, sweet my Love, I die for thee,
I die in thy arms, Love, ah me!"

The Lass I Love
(After a Few Cups of Port)

There is a lass I used to love,
      And whom I do love yet;
But she is far away from me,
      Nor ever have we met.

She is too high a being for me,
      A bride for gods to woo;
He made her, but so fair is she,
      He well might love her too.

It was my fate one fatal day,
      This fair maid to behold,
And since then, I have pined and wept,
      In secret tears untold.

How I have loved her, God knows well,
      If any God, there be; –
For now, methinks, this wide world has,
      No Guv'nor certainly.

Or if they say God surely is,
      Then this too must be told,
That either He is fast asleep,
      Or He has grown too old!

He's feeble now and powerless,
      His children suffer pain......
The sun burns hot, the wind blows dust,
      Defiant and insane.

I never met a heart that loved,
    But e'er his face was pale,
His eyes bedimmed, and on his lips
    Trembled a doleful tale.

Or even if a heart could joy,
    In love requited,
It was amid a thousand thorns,
    The poor thing had to tread……

But I have rambled in my pain,
    As I ne'er meant to do……
The moon sails bright, the clouds float fast,
    As I'd fain float up too.

But I am just a mass of clay,
    That never thus can fly;
My girl too is far, far away,
    Nor e'er can be nearby.

She cannot hear these distant moans,
    And bursts of wailful song,
And I must pine and weep in love,
    Until God knows how long!

"I'll Melt and Mingle in My Love"

The heavy, hanging mists of morn,
    Shroud all the plain in vapoury veil;
The pearl-drops cluster on my brows,
    My lashes, and my face so pale;

My arms are folded on my breast,
    My eyes closed, I drive on and on,
And dream along of things sad-sweet,
    And bliss that may be mine anon......

The sun's blaze bursts behind the mist,
    The mist like shifting sands does shift,
        I startled wake from my sweet dreams;
    The dew-drops on the boughs and leaves,
        Glisten pearl-wise in slant sun-beams.

And some will fall upon the ground,
    Some shine and tremble on the bough,
        Till all melt in the sun above;
    So, on the bough, or on the ground,
        I'll melt and mingle in my Love!

Spring Blossoms

Ye *neem* and *siris* blossoms,
    Born of the youthful year,
Your smell my brain suffuses,
    Diffusing sweetly far and near.

In stillness of the evening,
    And quiet of the dawn,
Your mild intoxication,
    Steals softly through the spirit on.

And then do ye transport me,
    Where love in me was born,
And where your balmy odours,
    Perfumed my love's old, misty morn.

And years are dead, and reborn,
    And ye have bloomed again;
But through the changing seasons,
    My sad love doth the same remain!

*Indian Lilac.
**Persian Silk or Mimosa.

But to Look Upon

Would not moment passed, but I did gaze,
    On something beautiful! A human form,
An aspect real, of a wondrous phase,
    A magic scene, be it a thunder-storm!
Or such, as paints the dreamful eye of Art,
    Gladsome or dreadful, but fantastic yet;
A face, in tender dreams might wrap the heart,
    Ay, aught to look upon if not to get.

My soul is hungry, doing nought I sit;
    Time passes o'er a life seems purposeless,
And wasteful, since no use is made of it, –
    Redundant rotting in its singleness!
Thus, seems it God! – for who can manifest
Thy purpose, and say it is not the best?

Before the *Granth Sahib

The priest in rhythmic, ringing tones,
    Chants forth the holy, scriptural hymn;
The ***sittar's* liquid, silver notes,
    Float on the air, and sink, and swim.

Filled by this ethereal chant,
    And moved by holy minstrelsy,
My eyes burst forth in gushing grief,
    My soul in tearful melody:
Recalling its unhappy love,
    My soul, O Love, thus weeps for thee!

*Sacred Scriptures of the Sikhs.
**Sittar/Sitar - Stringed instrument used in Indian classical music.

In the Skies

Oft when I've slept, I have flown in the skies,
> And I wonder 'tis how,
> I cannot do it now!

I've felt such a pleasant sensation of peace,
> Of coolness so pure,
> Not of Earth, I am sure.

No effort I made but I flew with mere thought,
> Though I feared to remain,
> Beyond black clouds of rain.

From the top of a house to another I flew,
> And I wonder 'tis how,
> I cannot do it now!

O, my spirit perhaps was thus flew in the sky,
> While these limbs here did rest,
> In the bed to their best.

How I long now for Death, I may fly where I like;
> This body is a mass,
> And so heavy, alas!

I cannot in the sky, while it clings to me, fly!
> I would fly to my Love,
> In Heaven above!

How free, then how free, from this bondage of frame!
> How free, O, how free,
> Like a bird on a tree!

The Earth and the Space and the Sky I would pace,
>   The world will have grown,
>   Then how vast and my own!

O come, sweet Death come and take me to your home!
>   I'm restless to pace,
>   In that wonderful place!

Fragments

I
"Some Time Ago"

Some time ago, I felt as though,
    I could not love again,
But now I feel a fever steal,
    Upon my brain!

II
"On Returning from a Visit to a Dear Old Place"

Alone I came, alone I went,
By love alone there I was sent:
A cloudy day today it is,
A day for us to love and kiss!

III
"Lines Written on a Small Picture of a Boy with a Harp"

Look where'er thou wilt,
    Each man has a harp; –
A harp in hand, or harp in eyes,
Or hidden in the heart it lies!

The Crescent and the Star

O crescent and the star,
How fair, how fair ye are!
I saw ye both ethereal bright,
The star within the crescent's light,
A night of th' early moon upon,
When in the sombre west ye shone.

And thus, ye looked so fair above,
A sight of Beauty, sight of Love:
Thou star, the blushing bride, within
Th' encircling arms, so firm but thin,
Of thee, O moon, celestial lover,
Under thy spacious, skyey bower.

And well is it that *they*
Have worshipped to this day,
Ye crescent and the star divine,
That in the sky sublimely shine,
Rare sight of Beauty, sight of Truth,
Your beauty shows the Truth in sooth!

The Mohammedans, whose religious emblem is the Crescent and the Star.

Daily Gifts

I've cast the last look on her face,
    Love's daily gifts are o'er; –
The daily gifts of glances few,
    Beyond I'll get no more!

Thy gifts, O Love, all vanish soon;
    Each is a lightning seen,
That brightens but for moment one,
    And then, – it had not been!

On Seeing a Clay-Relief of *Radha and Krishna

Thy happy love, Lord, makes me weep,
    Thy love for Thine own Radha dear;
While I my lonely vigils keep,
    And palely in love languish here.

Thy soft-eyed Radha so nearby,
    Clasped gently to Thy loving breast;
While thus Thy love-lorn servant, I,
    Do pine for such celestial rest;
Vouchsafe me Master, fallen low,
The joy Thou once on earth didst know!

---

*Revered Hindu deities and divine lovers.

Withdrawn

I had loved her these days in secret and pain,
    Too shy to tell her the same;
I loved her and longed, but thought it all vain,
    And fed my sad heart on her name!

But last night I sat on the threshold, I dreamt,
    While my Love stood over my head,
And gazed at my hair that were all unkempt,
    With her arms on the panels full-spread.

I felt her keen gaze, and my head did I raise,
    And looked in her face, all fair!
And how soft, O, how soft were those eyes and their gaze,
    Like the eyes of a deer they were!

O, I lingered my gaze on her beautiful face,
    And I stretched my arms out, full blest!
And something in my heart seemed to fly from its place,
    To take its abode in her breast!

She bent her fair form and kissed my wet eye, –
    Then swiftly she fled with a scream,
And left me forlorn and too o'erful to cry,
    So, I got up, – but found it a dream!

O, what a delight and bliss, my heart,
    That kiss sent a thrill through my soul!
O, was it not fragrant that kiss my heart,
    A Heaven complete and whole?

The Parrots on the *Peepul Tree

A fight of parrots once I saw,
>They billed their feed unfettered, free,

Upon a pile of golden grain,
>Under an emerald *peepul* tree.

On drawing nigh, I startled them, –
>Their ears as e'er alert agree, –

And with a green and beauteous swoop,
>Were all lost in the green o' the tree......

And thus, upon the worldly Pile,
>We feed under th' Eternal Tree;

Till startled once by watchful Time,
>We fly unto Eternity;

**Again descend, again ascend,
>And thus, from Time to Time it be;

Till, satiate with worldly Grain,
>We mingle in Eternity!

---

*Peepal Tree: Ficus religiosa or sacred fig tree native to the Indian subcontinent and having religious significance in Hinduism, Buddhism, Sikhism, and Jainism.
**A reference to the Hindu doctrine of Transgression of Souls.

The Rural Nymph

That village washer-maiden,
    Upon the village tank,
Is beating with her hammer of wood,
    Her linen on the bank.

Then wringing all her bundle:
    The gowns and skirts each one,
She trips, and hangs them on the hedge,
    To dry them in the sun.

And waiting for her mother,
    To fetch more clothes from home,
Upon the bank in idle sport,
    She sits, until she come;

And dips her milk-white ankles,
    Within the stream to cool,
And draws such wondrous, magic lines,
    Deep in the limpid pool.

And now she softly plunges,
    Her limbs within the stream,
And bathes with silver arms, and looks,
    A mermaid of a dream.

The water round her clinging, –
    Round all her drenched charms, –
It greets its love-nymph to its home,
    In liquid, melting arms......

And bathing in that water,
> I feel a strange delight:
That self-same stream does hold me, which,
> Does hold that water-sprite.

The ripples dance around her,
> And kiss that nymph in glee; –
Those very ripples traverse far,
> They come and they kiss me!

The End

It is an ageless, soundless dream.
    Of finest mould......
Far... far... wrapt it doth seem,
    Ten millionfold!

All lost in One Eternal Love,
    One Perfect Bliss...
No word, no sound, no space, no move, –
    No touch, no kiss!

But close... so close... in slumber deep,
    Head unto head...
Love's End... Eternal End and Sleep...
    Both eternal wed!

The Search

As Night around the Earth doth roll,
    In silent search of Sun,
So e'er deceived, my wandering soul,
    Doth seek the Unseen One.

And as doth Night, in Paradise,
    With Light Eternal blend,
My soul here baffled, there will rise,
    And join the Unknown End!

To the Twinkling Star

O, thou star, thus twinkling far,
Thou wondrous, scintillating star,
Thy shimmering of diamond hues:
From pinks to purples, greens to blues, –
My soul sees visions vast in thee,
Delicious dreams of phantasy!

The Forlorn Flute
(After the Persian)

Hark to the distant, plaintive note,
      The wild and wailing flute complain,
Unto all winds around that float,
      A secret plain:

"Oh, from my native soil torn,
      Where with my Love entwined, I stood,
Some ruthless hand has cut, and borne,
      Me to this wood."

"And so, my pining heart hath found,
      Through intense anguish, moaning tongue, –
My reed burst forth in piteous sound,
      Thus, long hath sung."

"Ye winds of east, ye winds of west,
      Upon your airy breasts I rove,
A wandering voice, in doleful quest
      Of long-lost Love."
      ....

My sundered soul thus flute-like cries,
      With woeful voice in wilderness. –
An echoing voice at last replies...
      My soul to bless!

"'Twas Only a Rose"

'Twas only a rose in the rose-bush,
    He was gazing at, on the lawn;
He stood with his eyes both close-fixed,
    And his arms behind him drawn.

He stood with a face full of sorrow,
    Intent on the half-blown rose,
Till he heaved a sigh of a sudden,
    Then slowly his eyes did close!

And still he stood as a statue,
    His head not a whit did rise,
From a deep, soul-deep meditation,
    Until rolled two big drops from his eyes!

And the rose had paused in wonder,
    Why tears at its sight should start?...
And he turned his steps from the rose-bush, –
    For Beauty but saddens the heart!

The Beauty of the Rose

Thy blushing beauty, rose,
With youthful, crimson glows,
    But makes me sad;
Thy loveliness doth fill,
My soul with sorrow still,
    Though thou art glad.

Why all thy beauty, rose,
My heart in sadness throws, –
    A stricken dove?......
My spirit sees in thee,
Far greater mystery:
    My beauteous Love.

Thy modest blush and meek,
But shows a fairer cheek –
    My heart well knows;
Thy fragrance doth but tell,
Of softer, sweeter smell:
    My sweetest Rose.

Thy beauty doth reflect,
The Beauty it can't get –
    My longing soul;
And hence with pain it fills,
And for the Beauty thrills:
    My lovely Goal.

On the Coming of the Rain

The night is close, and all the air is still;
    Blue streaks of smoke wreathe all the village round,
    And from a roof a dog's dull, yelping sound;
Belated herd's home-coming tinkling shrill;
    The glow-worm's twinkle sailing on is found;
The shrouded moon in th' *omen-ring* doth thrill;
And many a far-off, blazing, luminous hill,
    Of clouds, aglow with lightning tongues abound.

And now the dark clouds gather; thunder roars,
    With growling groans afrom the vapour-peaks;
    Then sweeps a blast with howling demon-shrieks,
Til with a final crash a torrent pours.
And soon it settles down to bounteous rain,
And on the thirsty Earth reigns peace again.

A circle of vapour round the moon, indicative to the Indian mind of impending calamity.

After the Rain

The rain doth cease; the eastern breeze –
    She breathes a drunken tale;
And in the sky the black clouds fly,
    Borne on the wings o' the gale.

The victor sun – he laughs in fun,
    At coward-clouds thus flee;
And jocund birds in airy herds
    Do dance about for glee.

The streams do flow, all singing low,
    Their melting hearts to prove;
All things are green that may be seen,
    New-dressed to meet their Love.
    ....

But I alone do sigh and moan,
    And all these beauties cloy;
For poor my heart is far apart,
    From all its only Joy!

Eyes Need Eyes

What care I aught for thy charms, O World?
    I cannot enjoy them alone!
To me thou art as a dreary land,
    Where only sand is blown...
    And I am a-weary grown!

The purple glow of the morning sun,
    The pendent pearls on the boughs,
And the joyous notes of waking birds,
    With which the heart would carouse,
    Do now but sad thoughts arouse!

Thou hast no doubt grand hills to show,
    And valleys of Paradise,
Where waters music-making flow,
    That fill us with glad surprise, –
    Yet alas!... for eyes need eyes!

Youth and Beauty

Why does that girl with pretty grace,
     Passing along the village way,
     Stop short aside, and shyly stay,
And under her hem half-hide her face,
The while I softly ride along,
Within my heart a lonely song?

And why does then that pretty maid,
     Behind her veil half-parted peep,
     And raise her large, white eyes, and deep,
So timidly with upturned head,
The while I softly cross her way,
And look upon that way-side fay?......

For she is young, and she is fair,
     And Youth and Beauty in her fill,
     Her bosom with a longing thrill,
And from her draw a stealthy stare,
At me, the while I pass and part,
That lingering look within my heart!

Loneliness

O loneliness!
    Hound after timid unspoken love!
        Thou silent ghost-like hound!
O merciless!
Thou born of hell's own womb,
More silent than a mid-night tomb, –
    A tomb 'mid tombs, beyond God's bound,
        Fearful e'en to the stars above!

If I Were the Sea

What joy would it be if I were the sea!
I would strike the rocks and bruise myself,
And yet I would laugh in glee!

Like a pirate, by force,
With thunders and roars,
I would sink the ships down,
And taking their store,
I would scatter it o'er.

And when my Love came,
To sail in a boat,
No boatman she'd need,
I would keep it afloat,
And drive it along,
With a rapturous song,
And safe in a headlong speed!

I would show her views,
Of charming hues,
Of clouds in the deeps above!
The breezes would blow,
All softly and slow,
And lull her with songs of love!

And when it grew dark,
I would drive back the bark,
And land her on shore; –
And as she went o'er,
I would breathlessly watch,
Her tripping along,

Till I saw her no more!
Then slowly would I turn,
A different song to learn, –
Now a sad, wailing song!

But when of a day,
I spied her on the beach,
I would gather the store,
I had scattered before,
And fondly to greet,
Her, in my own speech,
I would rush to the beach,
Where – softening to a lap and a beat,
I'd place it at her feet!

The Breeze and the Cloud

I

The breeze that softly comes,
    And woos with sweet caress,
An eager tune she hums,
And whispers, "We are loving chums,"
    With clinging, keen embrace.

But whence the breeze – she blows,
    In sly, seductive race,
And whither madly goes,
How many more she woos, – she knows,
    And who has seen her face?

II

The cloud that swiftly flies,
    The cloud that slowly sails,
On airy plinth it lies, –
A magic castle in the skies,
    And tells us fairy-tales.

But the cloud so wondrous fair,
    Has ever-fickle forms,
And naught but smoke and air;
Now plenteous rain on breast does bear,
    Now breeder of the storms.
....

And so, the gentle breeze and cloud,
    So sweet and lovely, fair of face. –
The breeze, a fickle Beauty proud,
The cloud a Tyrant roaring loud,
    Make moral for Man's changefulness.

Lotus Blooms

Within the paddy field,
    A cool and breezy morn,
Along the banks and *bunds* I rove,
    And all forlorn.

My listless eyes awake,
    At yon Beauty in the pond:
A host of water-lilies twined,
    In sisterly bond.

A host of water-lilies,
    All bathing in the sun,
And dreaming like same languid nymphs,
    Of their Loved One.

Within love's ocean-depth,
    Their yearning souls are steeped;
Their golden, glowing hearts alone,
    Above have peeped.

Mid shyly opening buds,
    Their weary vigils kept;
On tear-dropped lotus leaves full-spread,
    Have lilies wept.

They're farther in the pool,
    All growing out of grasp; –
Thus, things of beauteous Mystery,
    Evade the clasp.

*Agricultural embankments.

But they are fair, too fair,
      And I stoop to try my luck,
I reach my stick – I stumble in; –
      But one I pluck.

And then I smell my prize, –
      A musky smell does shed; –
I smell in it my fragrant Love,
      My Lotus-Maid!

Aspiration

O Shelly, Wordsworth, Keats!
    Where are your spirit gone?
Draw my own spirit that beats,
    With yours in unison.

Fain, would I leave for aye,
    This frame, with you to roam,
Through regions far away,
    High, high up in the dome!

My spirit also sings,
    Similar songs of love,
And has its wanderings,
    In starry realms above.

When these limbs lie in sleep,
    It flies, but then — alas!
It comes back and I weep,
    When nightly hours all pass!

Would I could freely roam,
    Through Earth and Sky and Deep?
I'd make no spot my home,
    Would laugh and sing and weep!

A Lullaby

(To the Sleeping Beauty)

Sleep, sleep my Love in the arms of the dawn,
With a peaceful, angelic face sleep on,
In thy silken coverlet full-length drawn,
While early-risen I am gazing upon......
    Sleep, sleep my Love!

Sleep, sleep my Love in the arms of the breeze,
That kisses thy eyes and thy limbs to ease,
Vain longings of wakeful hours all cease,
And thy soul in slumberland finds release......
    Sleep, sleep my Love!

Sleep, sleep my Love in the arms of a dream,
Where under love's caressing moonlit beam,
Beside love's whispering, woodland stream,
We two, all alone, do glide and gleam......
    Sleep, sleep my Love!

The Huller's Song

That girl has come to the hulling-yard,
 With the skin of pearl,
After many a day to the hulling-yard, –
 It is my girl.

Welcome my girl to the winnowing-ground,
 'Mid the grindstone's whirl,
We'll winnow together in the winnowing ground,
 Side by side my girl.

Together we'll turn the grinding-stone;
 And where the grains twirl,
We'll see sweet sights in the grinding-stone,
 Face to face my girl.

Rift in the Lute

'Tis superb, ravishing! All Earth and Sky!
    Beauteous as nothing is, – a paradise!
    Yet-oh, 'tis charming only to the eyes!
For from my soul yet breaks a heavy sigh!
These lovely aspects cannot satisfy;
    It seeks those joysome dreams to realise,
    Wherein "thas smiles for smiles and sighs for sighs,
And thoughts are echoed back in full reply!

These ebon clouds that pompous upward sail,
    All in one vast procession – young and old;
    This Nature's fondling, fitful, romping breeze,
That carries now and then a broken tale......
    O such sights are enchanting to behold,
    Yet they the sadness of my soul increase!

The Swallow on the Lake

*The *Jacob banks are green –*
Thick carpets spread between
The columned, sturdy *babul* trees –
Those Nature's shady canopies.

An Autumn afternoon,
When palely shines the moon,
And swallows come in sable bands –
Those emigrants from distant lands, –

A swallow twittering,
Its black plumes fluttering,
Is wagging her forked, restless tail,
Within its little heart a wail;

Self-poised in the air,
And with a steady stare,
Deep in the bosom of the lake –
Some vision of her heart to wake:

Within its depth per-chance,
She sees her Love advance,
With open wings to meet its mate,
That anxious-eyed above doth wait.

And soon to taste the bliss –
Her new-found Love to kiss,
She swiftly on the lake drops down, –
The vision breaks – it was her own!

*'Jacob Talao (Lake)' is an expanse of water at the foot of the Hyderabad hill, towards the north, a beauty-spot named after a beneficent officer.

She tries again, again,
Her new-found Love to gain;
Till baffled at the close of day,
With wearied wings she goes away.

The Poet's Soul

I

A frantic mood,
And yet subdued;
The confined soul,
Will sweep control,
And rise and soar,
And sweetly pour,
A melody,
Full mournfully!

Now raging, now mild,
Now rapturous wild,
Now crying like a child,
Now ceasing to weep,
And falling to sleep.

Now rising with a moan,
    Too piercing and paining,
Now falling with a groan,
    Helplessly complaining.

II

But the voice of the wind,
Is calling behind,
And forgetting its sorrow,
And swift like an arrow,
Away to the skies,
    Fast sweeping the main,
An eagle – it flies,
    Once again!

There sailing with a cloud,
Or the stars among,
She sings a wild song,
In sad rapture and loud.

III

She knows not the time,
Of any other clime,
But her own, her own sad chime.
Be it night, be it day,
In stormy array,
Or ever so gay,
She is singing away!
Be it Autumn, be it Spring,
She will never cease to sing,
Of a happy or sad thing.

Thus, ever in a trance,
She will madly advance,
And on a strain chance,
Keeping tune with a dance,
And our sadness enhance.

Thus, ever does she sing,
In cage or on the wing.

The Moon-Lit Stream

The sunset twilight was gone,
And the rising full-moon shone,
On the breast of *Fuleli* stream,
With many an opal beam.
And the broad, white belt of light,
Across the river, so bright,
Seemed a bridge of silver thrown,
For the Poets – spirits grown.

And girt by that silver belt,
A glistening mermaid dwelt, –
For the shimmering ripples shone,
Like scales of a fish in the sun.
And the sparkling ripple-crests –
They did heave their shining breasts,
And murmured, and laughed, and danced,
And with twinkling eyes they glanced.
In that belt of silver essence,
Was a dreamy efflorescence.

And currents from this and that side,
Like streaks of light did they glide,
And merged and mingled full bright,
In the central Stream of Light.

---

*'The Fuleli', the canal-river of Sindh, flowing through the heart of Hyderabad, with its beauteous windings and its garden-banks.

Across the Sea

Across the moon-lit plain,
    Over the silver sea,
Beyond the sight of men,
    O Love, my soul sees thee:
Upon thy terrace fair,
    Above the shining sea,
Thou standest and dost stare,
    Across the sea at me!

Till You Arrive

Will you show me your face, my Love?
    Will you show me your face?
Your face from the window above,
    Just for a moment's space?

I will whisper a word, my Love,
    A word, and then I'm dumb,
To say that I wait for you, Love,
    Wait, and will wait till you come!

I will wait for Æons, my Love,
    Through Life, through Death, I'll wait,
O till you arrive, my Love,
    Till you pass through my gate!

Music Wails

O pause, sad singer! Cease thy rending strains,
    Full swelling in a long beseeching wail!
Ay pause! Thy voice, minstrel, keenly pains!
    Thy notes up-carrying a mournful tale,
Do seem so many grief-stricken airy things,
    Ceaselessly sailing through the space above:
Thin widowed voices on broken wings,
    Consuming with an ever-burning love!......

They've died away at last; – kind Night doth wreathe,
    Perhaps, her sleep-bestowing arms round thee!
But hark! Those strains, though hushed, yet soundless breathe,
    A softer and a vaster melody!
Sleep, sleep, fond lover! May such love be blest,
With never-ending happiness and rest!

The Bird and the Beast

The swallow oft alights,
    On the black back of the buffalo; –
In black things he delights,
    He loves his kindred colour so.
The swallow loves to perch,
    On the broad back of the buffalo; –
In usual, weary search,
    Of frail tree-tops he need not go.

He likes the stable earth,
    And is borne along from mead to mead,
Unconscious of his mirth,
    She browses in her lazy speed......

Thus, Bird and Beast are bound,
    And Creation's common kinship tell;
Thus, Air and Earth are found,
    To mingle; and all, all is well!

The Rose and its Thorns

Last eve I pruned the rose-bush,
    With all my tender love and care;
But the thorns pricked and scratched me,
    Their pain did faintly linger there.

I wondered why the rose-bush,
    Thus, paid me for my love and care; –
But where the thorns did pain me,
    The rose's sweetness lingered there!

The Simplest Things

I

A shining shell plucked from the sands,
    With whispering music-sound;
A pebble picked from rock or plain,
    Rain-beaten, smooth, and round;
Wild flowers from the *brier*-bush,
    Through brambles sought and found;
The simplest things my sweetness claim,
    Love, gathered in thy sacred name!

II

I put the shell within my breast,
    That thrills with secret pleasure;
I place the pebble in my desk,
    And deem it my best treasure;
I wreathe the wild flowers for thy neck,
    And they turn sweet past measure; –
Precious are plainest things to me,
    Love, treasured in thy memory!

*Brier or Briar: Thorny plants that form thickets such as the rose bush.

The Initiated Devotee

What a magic is Thine, O Master,
    I see with wonder and joy!
What pipe dost thou play all hidden,
    To strike the ears of a boy?

How beautiful are these colours,
    That fall on the naked screen!
So many and yet all different, –
    O say what they all do mean!

Thou playest Thy pipe for ever,
    Nor stoppest a minute to smile.
At the wonder Thy magic produces, –
    O show Thyself for a while!

I know not to sing Thy praises,
    Thou who art a Mystery complete;
I see all Beauty before me,
    And I prostrate at Thy feet.

A Cup of Cocoa

The sun is setting through my window bars,
    Behind the *babul* tree-top, with a dip,
In the horizon's rim, as I recline,
    Within my easy-chair, and vaguely sip,
    A steaming cup of cocoa to my lip.

And wreathed by idly circling curls of steam,
    And lost in dream-cloud vapour, – my sad soul,
Is wreathed and lost in visions of old times,
    And distant memories do swiftly roll,
    In keen reality, vivid and whole:

When we took cocoa by the sunset sea, –
She poured it out, and made a cup for me.

Acacia nilotica or gum arabic tree or thorny acacia: Native to Africa, the Middle-East and the Indian subcontinent.

A Harlot's Heart
*(To the Air of an *Urdu Ghazal)*

Come, Love, this harlot's heart receive,
To thy reluctant heart, this eve:

When breezes, clouds, and rain from high,
Bespeak my love's sincerity;
For though a harlot's trade I own,
My heart has not a harlot's grown......
Come, Love, etc.

The moment thy heart throbbed to mine,
My way-ward love has been all thine;
From many it has merged in one,
As moon and stars are lost in Sun.......
Come, Love, etc.

I hate my life, my well-known name,
My beauteous self I view with shame;
Come, save me from this misery,
And make me thine, – thy slave to be!...
Come, Love, etc.

*An ancient form of rhythmic poetry originating in 7th-century Arabia and later spreading to the Indian subcontinent by Sufi mystics during the Ghaznavid (Persian) dynasty.

Love's Philosophy

Love, thou wilt surely come to me,
    In all thy freshness, all thy bloom;
For One Being dwells in thee and me,
    And He is drawn to His perfume.

In love I seek myself in thee,
    In love the Being Itself pursues;
In love I give thyself to thee,
    How canst thou thy own self refuse?

At the Double-Door

Within the shadow of the double door,
      Her bare arm on the panel-top full-spread,
      Her snow-white muslin veil upon her head,
She stood, whom I had hoped to see no more.
And down below her door-steps, there I stood,
      Full in the flood of moon-light, on the road,
      And gazed up at her, where she faintly showed,
A dusky, sylph-like shade, all pure and good.

I could not see her face, I only heard,
      In response to my greeting shyly weak,
      The music of few accents modest, meek,
And then she turned away without more word.
She did not take me in her holy presence, –
But on her threshold, I paid my obeisance!

"For Ever, and For Ever"

I

No need of pearl or gem,
Or golden diadem; –
Mine be the 'necklace of her arms',
A pair of living ivory charms,
Thrown round my yielding neck,
To nobly deck, For ever, and for ever.

II

Frail are those *champak* flowers,
And all the jasmine bowers; –
Give me the rose-bud of her mouth,
With odours culled from East and South,
Laid on my longing lips,
With nectar-sips,
For ever, and for ever.

III

All Piety and Faith,
Vain refuge, – so Love saith; –
For me, the haven of her breast,
Soft shelter of repose and rest;
O would my troubled head,
Thereon were laid,
For ever, and for ever!

*Magnolia Champaca - a fragrant flower native to Southeast Asia.

"How Beauteous Is the World, Yet Oh How Lonely"

How beauteous is the world, yet Oh how lonely!
These rocks do make me joyful, yet how vast,
And dismal is the gulf betwixt us twain, –
That of unlikeness! ... Ignorant, fluttering soul,
And mute, huge masses full of mystery!
O speak! Why are ye dumb, grand, wondrous rocks?
The trees upon your crests and bosoms vast,
Do nod and sway and fearless sport with winds,
But never speak a word with human beings!
Of what avail then this poor power of man?
O speak to me and tell me all your tales,
Of whom in an ecstatic play did plan,
Your view-defying heights! Of all ye know,
Of Him who's out of human sight; and say,
If ye can see Him, ye that have no sight?

Ye've made a joyous company of your own,
Ye, with these ever-falling cataracts,
And yielding maiden-dales; young, blooming groves,
And clouds and breezes cool! – too, too complete,
To crave for cruel, fickle human ties!
Blest chosen ones! That know no grief or sorrow!
O would I too were a thing of living joy:
A cloud, a flower, a stream, in your quiet world,
And I would seek no more to learn the Truths,
With which I rack and trouble now my brain!

Prof. M.U. Malkani

The eldest son of *Raisahib Udharam Malkani, Mangharam,* or *Dada Mangha* as we would fondly call him, was born on December 24, 1896, in *Hyderabad, Sindh*. He was fascinated with the works of *Aldous Huxley, Honoré de Balzac, Leo Tolstoy, Émile Zola, Thomas Hardy,* and many other western novelists, and had little interest in taking over the reins of *zamindari* from his father. That responsibility fell upon his younger brother *Alimchand Malkani*. To pursue a career in literature, *Mangharam* gave up his ancestral vocation and became a professor of English at *D. J. Sind College, Karachi*.

In 1923, *Prof. M.U. Malkani* and his friend *Khanchand Daryani* established the *Rabendarnath Tagore Literary and Dramatic Club of Sindh,* inaugurated by the great *Bard of Bengal, Rabindranath Tagore* himself. During his time in *Karachi,* he wrote 34 one-act plays and 4 full-length plays, leading to the appellation *"The Grand Old Man of Sindhi Literature"*. Not only did he direct the plays himself, but he also sometimes acted in them. Consequently, in 1933, he received the opportunity to star in a *Hindi* movie titled *Insaan Ya Shaitan,* directed by *Moti Gidwani*. He played the lead role in the film opposite *Jaddanbai*, the mother of the celebrated actress *Nargis*.

After the partition, *Prof. M.U. Malkani* migrated to *India* where he co-founded *Jai Hind College, Bombay,* in 1948, and served with great distinction, as a professor of English until the day he retired. He also started specialized literary classes in 1949 at the *Sindhi Sahit Mandal (Sindhi Literary Society),* where aspiring poets and short story writers would gather to present their writings for evaluation and constructive criticism. It is said that this initiative, which lasted 14 years, gave a new lease of life towards the preservation of the *Sindhi* language. It helped young writers rediscover their cultural identity, engage with the community, and find their feet in the vastly unfamiliar and uncertain socio-political landscape after the partition – which had prised them from their beloved homeland.

In the year 1956, *Prof. M.U. Malkani* led a delegation of *Sindhi* writers to the *Asian Writers' Conference, New Delhi,* where he impressed upon *Dr Rajendra Prasad,* the first President of India, that the *Sindhi* language be acknowledged in the *8th Schedule of the Indian Constitution* and be ranked equally with the other recognized languages. This pioneering effort culminated in the *Sindhi* language getting its due recognition and acceptance on April 10, 1967. He founded the *Sindhi Adabi Sangat (Sindhi Literary Fraternity)* and also served as the president of the *Sindhi Sahit Mandal.* He wrote more than 22 books, including *Sindhi Nasar Ji Tarikh (History of Sindhi Prose),* for which he received the *Sahitya Akademi Award* (the highest literary honour bestowed by the Indian government) in 1969. He was also awarded a *Sahitya Akademi Fellowship* in 1972, the only *Sindhi* writer thus honoured so far.

An eminent scholar, critic, writer, playwright, and literary historian, he was indeed a towering figure of *Sindhi* literature. With his demise on December 1, 1980, we lost a much-loved family member; and the community, its national treasure.

References

Rajpar, Qasim. *Father of Sindhi One Act Play, Prof Mangha Ram Malkani.* www.academia.edu, 2015. *https://www.academia.edu/10705733/Father_of_Sindhi_One_Act_Play_Prof_Mangha_Ram_Malkani.*

Mangharam Udharam Malkani. *Wikipedia: The Free Encyclopedia.* Wikimedia Foundation, last modified November 26, 2023. *https://en.wikipedia.org/wiki/Mangharam_Udharam_Malkani.*

تیر کائیندا رہندا
گُوڑھا وہندا رہندا

Teer Khaate Jayenge
Aasoon Bahaate Jayenge

*Transcribed from a handwritten scribble on the back of the original copy, hailing the act of perseverance in the face of adversity while pursuing one's mission, or as per the theme of this book, one's soulmate. It is important to mention the existence of a popular song with the same title that was featured in the 1952 Hindi film Deewana, sung by Lata Mangeshkar with music composed by Naushad.

Made in United States
Orlando, FL
05 January 2025